Wait, Don't Forget!

This book was printed in the original/Asian format. Please read panels from right to left.

**Saint Sophia Girls' School
First Year Monastic Class,
Emily Sakuraba**

There is the Monastic Class for sisterhood training in addition to the regular class Ayano and the others belong in Saint Sophia Girls' School, and Emily is a nun apprentice there. She was added as Ayano's rival, so look out for their fight over Kamioda.

She dotes on Miss Reiko and joined the club for her. She is open-natured and very easy for me to manipulate that I enjoy drawing her. She is my favorite character.

POUT

She is a common, laid-back lady. She is predictable yet less impressionable, and positive but lacks presence. I realize I should have done more with her.

Saint Sophia Girls' School Sewing Club President, Mai Orimiya

Orimiya-san is a first-year student and is one year younger than Kamioda. She is a quiet, shy person, but she does cosplay as an incongruous hobby. She appears neat with her black bobbed hair and I personally like it.
No, I really love it.

Puri Puri, Vol.5 THE END

EVERYONE IN MY CLASS KNOWS BUT THEY WON'T EXPLAIN IT.

AND I CAN'T JUST ASK ANYONE ABOUT IT.

W-WELL, UH...

ACK...

HMM, SHE'S TESTING ME NOW!

SHE'S GIVING ME THIS SERIOUS LOOK I'VE NEVER SEEN.

Maybe it isn't a joke.

I CAN TELL YOU WHAT I KNOW.

...

B-BUT SHE IS IN NEED OF HELP.

I REALLY DON'T KNOW HOW.

I SHOULDN'T BE THE ONE TO EXPLAIN, THOUGH.

AUGHHH AUGHHH AUGHHH AUGHHH

STARE

IN THAT CASE, IF IT'S OKAY THAT I'M A PRIEST APPRENTICE, I'D BE HAPPY TO HELP YOU.

GLIMMER

GLIMMER

WELL, UM...

N-NOTH-ING.

WHAT'S WRONG?

?

IS THAT RIGHT?

S-SEX?!!

まじっ

SERIOUS

PLEASE TEACH ME HOW TO HAVE SEX!!

I'M GOING TO TELL FATHER SHINGU. ♡

BOINK

A PRIEST APPRENTICE SHOULDN'T GIVE PERVERTED LOOKS. ♡

GASP

YOU WERE LOOKING AT MY CHEST, WEREN'T YOU?

BOINK BOINK

BOINK BOINK

THAT'S ENOUGH TEASING!

BAH

CLAK

G-GOOD EVENING. ♡

UFU FU FU FU. ♡

SCOOT

WH-WHAT ARE YOU DOING HERE AT THIS HOUR?

EMILY?!

SNEAKING INTO YOUR ROOM, OF COURSE. ♡

WHY AM I HERE?

WHAT IS IT WITH HER? SHE SAID SHE IS A NUN APPRENTICE.

OH, BOY.

GRIN

BUT...

SHE WAS KIND OF CUTE.

She seems to like me, too.

EEE-YAHHH!

GORO GORO GORO
ROLL-ROLL

RUSTLE RUSTLE

THUD

CREAK CREAK

UM-PH! ♡

WH-WHO IS IT?

I'M HERE FOR ASCETIC TRAINING!

I MEAN, WHAT AM I THINKING?!

RATTLE

RATTLE

W-WE'RE
...

WHAT?!

HIS GIRLFRIEND?

WE'RE NOT IN THAT KIND OF RELATIONSHIP.

PANIC

PANIC

YOU, YOU...

SHO——CK

I LIKE KAMIODA-KUN. ♡ HE'S SO FUNNY. ♡

THEN I CAN DO WHATEVER I WANT.

OH.

WHAT ARE YOU DOING?!

WHA-WHA-WHA-WHA...

ARGH

BAM

SAY...

YOU'VE BEEN COMPLAINING ABOUT ME.

POINT?

WHAT IS YOUR RELATION TO HIM?

PUNCH?

DON'T PLAY AROUND WITH KAMIODA-KUN!

FWIP

THOUGHT HE'D PRAY FOR HIS SINS AGAIN. ♪

Y-YOU SHOULDN'T SHOW OFF YOUR PANTIES...

HE IS BEING SERIOUS!

TWITCH

FLIP

TOO BAD, IT'S JUST A SKORT. ♡

YOU'RE RIGHT.

I HAVE TENNIS FIFTH PERIOD.

I'M EMILY SAKURABA, A FIRST YEAR/ FRESHMAN IN THE SAINT SOPHIA GIRLS' SCHOOL MONASTIC CLASS

YOU'RE GOOD! REAL FUNNY!!

WHAT'S YOUR NAME?

RECORD OF CONFESSIONS VOL.4

OH, YES, I KNOW YOU! KAMIODA THE ONLY GUY IN SCHOOL!

I-I'M MASATO KAMIODA.

...WEIRDO?

ZAP!

RECORD OF
CONFESSIONS
VOL. 4

BUT...

...I'M A
WEIRDO

DE ——— PRESSED

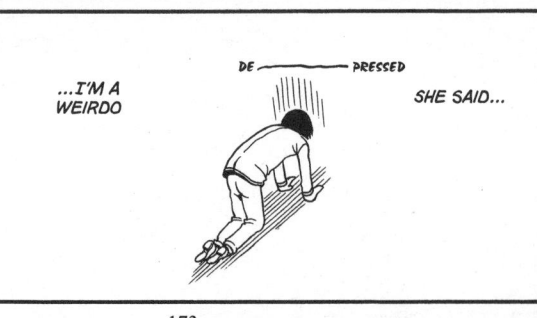

SHE SAID...

173

CH-CHURCH IS STRICT, HUH?

THROB
THROB
THROB

YOU POOR THING. ♡

STING
STING

OH, YES, WE HAVE A POLICY TO DO A SIMPLE INSPECTION OF YOUR POSSESSIONS.

MAY I HAVE A LOOK?

SURE!

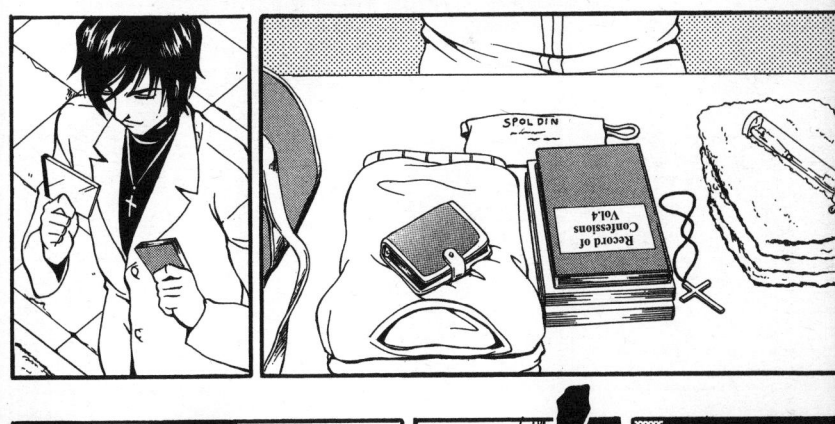

SPOL DIN

Record of Confessions Vol.4

UH... IS SOMETHING THE MATTER?

!!

FLAP

FLIP FLIP

OH, NOT REALLY.

I'VE SEEN YOUR REPORT CARD.

YOU'RE AN EXCELLENT STUDENT.

YOU WILL MAKE A GREAT PRIEST. KEEP UP THE GOOD WORK.

THANK YOU!

THAT WAS EXCELLENT. THOSE CHILDREN WERE VERY PLEASED.

AND LAST MONTH'S HALLOWEEN PERFORMANCE.

I'LL BE WORKING FOR HIM STARTING TODAY. HOW EXCITING!

WOW! HE'S COOL AND SEEMS LIKE A NICE PRIEST!

Thank God!

NICE OF YOU TO COME.

TH-THANK YOU!

I WILL DO MY BEST!

I WISH YOU THE BEST OF LUCK.

IKENOHATA SAINT SOPHIA CHURCH

WE WERE ABLE TO FORGE AHEAD WITH SCHOOL REFORM.

IT WOULD BE IDEAL TO HAVE THE STUDENTS ORGANIZE AND FOLLOW THE REGULATIONS.

THE NEW SCHOOL REGULATIONS WILL BE IN PLACE NEXT MONTH.

IN THE FUTURE, WE WILL RETURN THE DONATIONS AND HAVE A PROPER SCHOOL SYSTEM WITH GOOD MANAGEMENT.

PRIN-CIPAL...

HOWEVER, WE HAVE NO CHOICE WITH A SCHOOL MANAGEMENT INFLUENCED BY A HUGE DONATION FROM AOI GROUP.

#25 THE ROAD TO PRIESTHOOD THE SECOND COURSE

BRAVO!
BRAVOOO!

NICE WORK, EVERYONE!

THOSE TWO ARE SEEING EACH OTHER. DAMN YOU!

KAMIOOODAAA!!

WHAM

HUH?

TWO GIRLS WHOSE LOVE DIMINISHED BECAUSE OF KAMIODA HAVE FORMED A FRIENDSHIP.

SO THE HALLOWEEN PERFORMANCE ENDED UP A HUGE SUCCESS.

I DID IT. I DID IT, YAMASHIRO-KUN!

ALL RIGHT, WE DID IT!

IT'S A MIRACLE!

MISS SHIROGANEEE!

OH, GODDDD!!

YOU WERE WATCHING ME THE WHOLE TIME.

I DID MY BEST! I REALLY DID!!

WEREN'T YOU?!

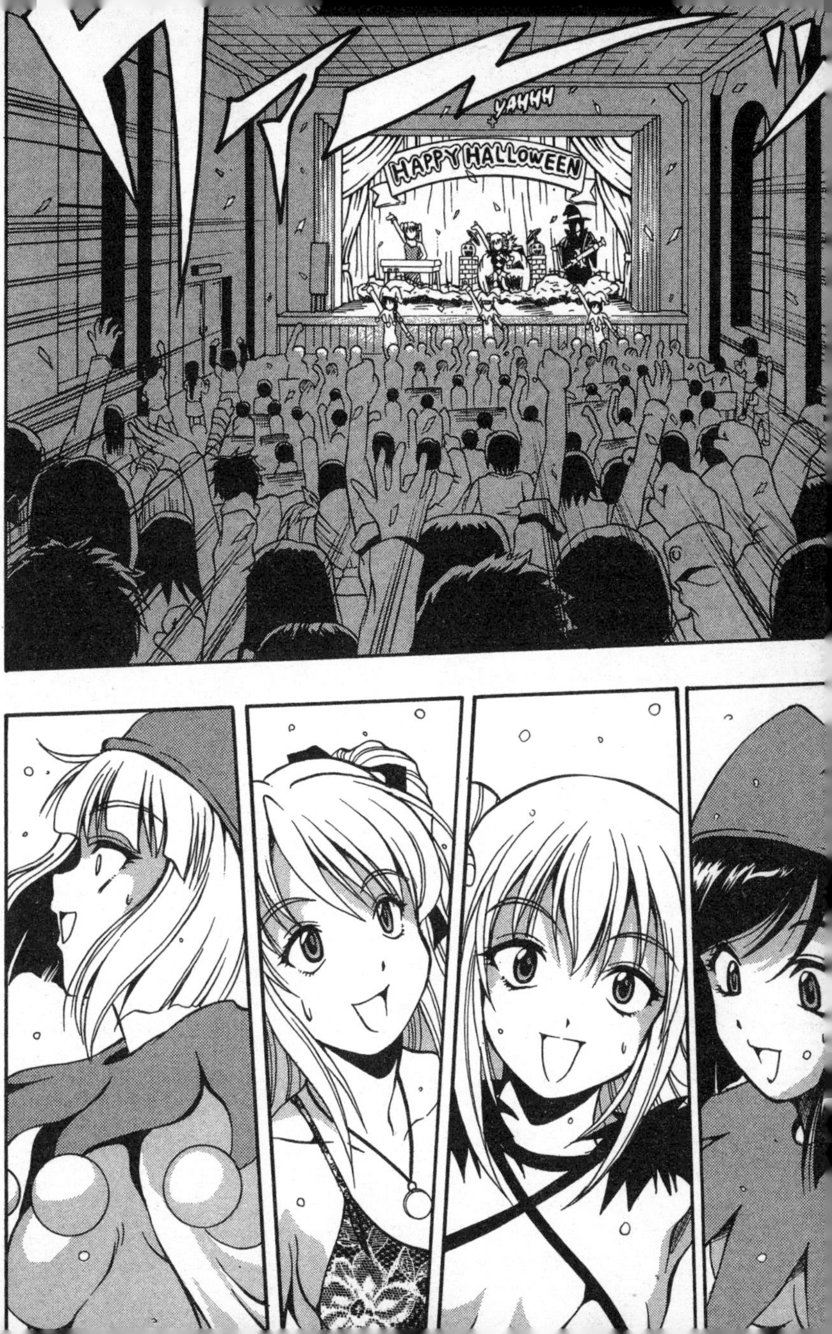
YAHHH
HAPPY HALLOWEEN

148

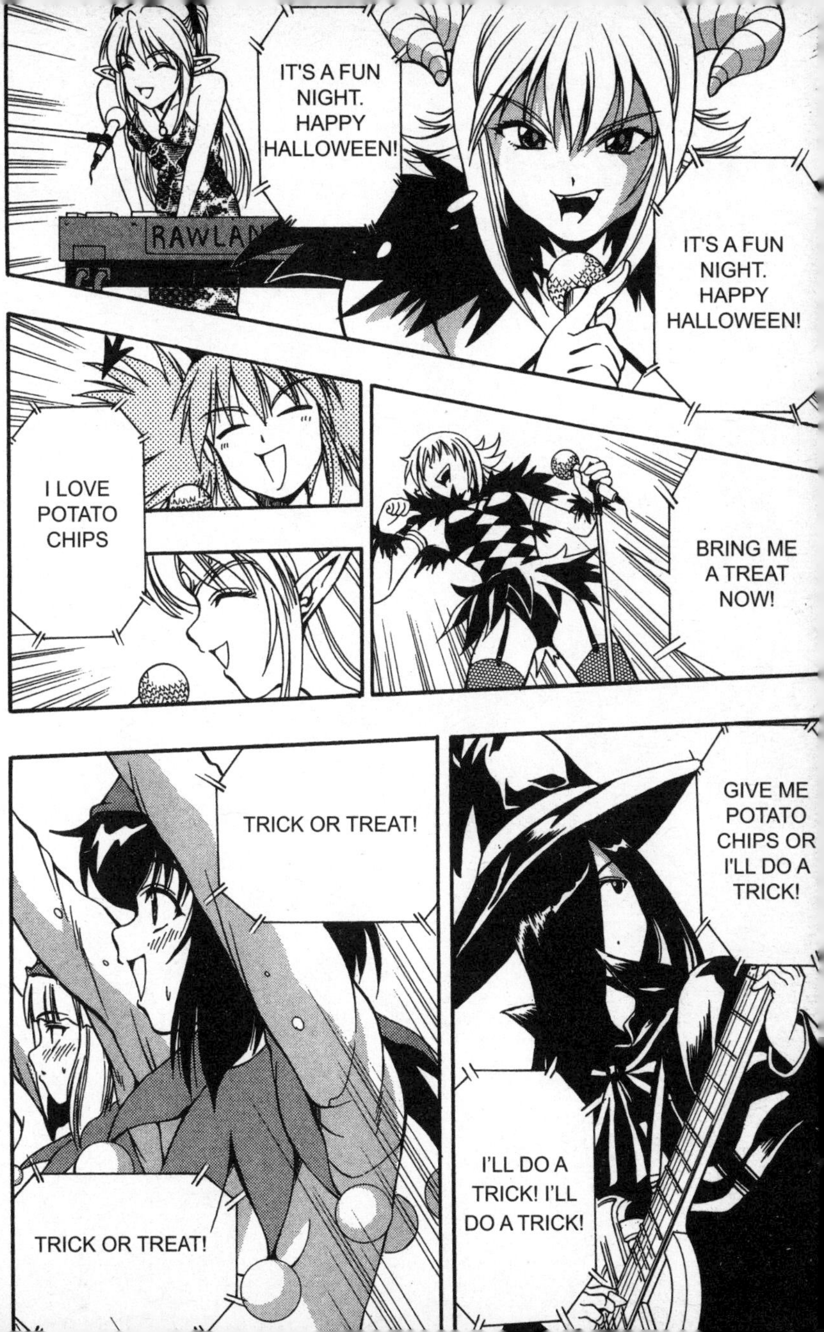

WE ALL WORKED HARD FOR THIS DAY.

REMEMBER OUR MISSION TO BRING DREAMS TO CHILDREN.

THIS IS MY LAST DAY WITH MISS SHIROGANE, HUH...

MUMBLE MUMBLE

A-ANYWAY...

...DO YOUR BEST, EVERYONE!

IF THIS IS OUR LAST DAY, MAYBE I SHOULD CONFESS TO YAMASHIRO-KUN AFTER THE EVENT.

THANK YOU FOR ALL YOUR HARD WORK.

UM...

UH, WELL...

WE ARE GOING LIVE TODAY.

WITH KAMIODA'S FRIENDS' HELP...

AFTER ALL THAT WAS SAID AND DONE...

THE PLAN WENT SMOOTHLY.

HALLOWEEN

PAY CLOSE ATTENTION ON YOUR HAND MOVEMENT IN DANCE.
THUMP
THUMP
KEEP YOUR BACK STRAIGHT.
YES, LIKE THAT.
AH! ♡
I can feel her chest.
SQUISH
SWING YOUR HIP ALONG.
RUB
さわ
RUB
さわ
AHH. ♡
YES, THAT'S GOOD. ♡
HAA.
HAA.
OH, YES, THIS FEELS GOOD. ♡

THIS IS GREAT!

IF I CAN SUSTAIN THIS, I CAN KEEP THOSE GIRLS UNDER CONTROL!

This will work!

IT CAN'T BE HELPED WITH THOSE GIRLS, THOUGH.

...BUT SUCCESS IS ALL IN HIS MIND NOW.

KAMIODA-KUN SAID HE WANTED TO ADVOCATE FOR COMMUNITY SERVICE...

HOW COME?
IT'S SEXY AND AWESOME!
WHY? IT'S NO GOOD FOR YOU?
I BET YOU'LL LOOK NICE AND ATTRACTIVE IN IT!
ZOOM
YOU KNOW, MADONNA WEARS SOMETHING MORE DARING IN CONCERT.
BESIDES, YOU HAVE A GREAT FIGURE FOR IT!
YOU THINK SO? HEE HEE HEE.

WHO IS DANCING?

WELL, SHE HASN'T DECIDED IF SHE WILL DO IT.

I'M VERY GOOD AT CHOREOGRAPHY. ♡

PANT PANT PANT PANT PANT

PLEASE TEACH ME STEP-BY-STEP, HEE HEE. ♡

ME, ME, ME! I'M DANCING!!

SHE REFUSED TO DANCE NO MATTER HOW HARD I BEGGED HER.

BUMP

WELL, YOU SEE, YOU ARE ALWAYS ARGUING AND REFUSING TO WORK TOGETHER.

NERVOUS

WE NEED TO PREVENT FAILURE OF THE EVENT BY ANY MEANS SO...

WHO'S ARGUING? WHO WOULDN'T WORK TOGETHER?

WHAT DO YOU MEAN?

HMM.

I GUESS I'LL HAVE TO ASK THEM.

HE'S BRINGING IN HELPERS FOR THE HALLOWEEN EVENT TODAY.

OH?

DID YOU HEAR ABOUT KAMIODA?

LEAD SINGER.

Multipurpose Room

LEAD SINGER.

IS THERE SOMEONE YOU CAN ASK TO FILL IN?

I KNEW IT WAS UNREALISTIC.

THAT'S WHAT I THOUGHT.

BUT WE DON'T HAVE MUCH TIME.

WE MAY NOT COMPLETE IT IN TIME IF WE LOOK FOR SOMEONE NEW.

I *DO* HAVE SOMEONE IN MIND.

YOU DO?!

W-WELL...

O-ORIMIYA-SAN.

YOU MEAN THOSE TWO.

IT'S A LITTLE UNREASONABLE TO WORK WITH THEM.

BASED ON WHAT I'VE SEEN, I THINK...

YOU PROBABLY SHOULD LOOK FOR OTHER HELP.

DASH DASH

WAHHHHHH!!

ﾌﾞﾙ
ﾌﾞﾙ
TREMBLE

ALIGH
...

AGGGH.

UM, WHAT'S THE MATTER?

ALIGH, DAMMIT!

I THINK THIS IS FINE.

ARE YOU DISSATISFIED WITH OUR AESTHETIC SENSE?

WHAT I'M TRYING TO SAY IS...

THAT DOESN'T LOOK MUCH LIKE A STONE WALL WITH THAT COLOR.

NO...

WHAT? ARE YOU TRYING TO NITPICK AT MY SINGING?

WHAT DO YOU KNOW ABOUT MUSIC? EH?

WELL, WHAT I MEAN IS...

I THINK YOUR SINGING SOUNDS TOO DEPRESSED.

I'M SORRY.

24 LET'S ENJOY HALLOWEEN!

RAHHH!!

THREE WEEKS UNTIL THE HALLOWEEN EVENT.

CATCH ME IF YOU CAN!

YOU'RE DEAD MEAT!

YOU WERE BOTH FERVENT. WELL DONE.

CLAP

114

WHAT A FIERCE BATTLE.

OH, WOW...

HOW CAN THEY BE SO SERIOUS AT IT?

BAM BAM BAM

IT'S ONLY THE CHICKEN FIGHT IN THE SPORTS FESTIVAL.

HAA.

HAA.

HAA.

HAA.

HAA.

WHY DON'T YOU ADMIT DEFEAT NOW?

HAA.

AUGH, ISN'T IT ABOUT TIME YOU SURREN- DERED?

HAA.

HAA.

HAH?

HOW FAST!

I HAVE EVEN SENT TWO PEOPLE TO THE HOSPITAL WITH MY SNATCH TECHNIQUE.

HEH HEH HEH.

THE FACT IS I WAS PREVIOUSLY A CHAIRPERSON OF THE HYAKUNIN ISSHU* CLUB.

* Hyakunin Isshu is in a card game where a reader reads a poem while the players scramble to find a card with a matching poem.

INTERESTING.

HEH!

THAT WAS CLOSE.

DAMN, I MISSED!

YOU ARE GOOD.

I THOUGHT YOU WERE JUST A GANG MEMBER.

BUT I HAVE...

...AN ULTIMATE TECHNIQUE AS WELL.

SWASH

SHUTO HYAKUNIN ISSHU GIRI!*

*Shuto Hyakunin Isshu Giri means, literally translated, "Knife Hand Hyakunin Isshu Cut." Translated as "one hundred poems from one hundred people," Hyakunin Isshu is a collection of cards with poems.

WHAT?

?!

ULTI-MATE!

UGH, NO FAIR THAT YOU GOT A WEAPON.
WHAT DO YOU MEAN, NO FAIR?!
RAHHH
YOU ATTACKED ME FIRST!
YOU TWO!
WEAPONS ARE NOT ALLOWED!
TROMP
TROMP
TROMP

THERE'S MY CHANCE!

KAPLUCK

NOTCHI!!

ROGER!

BAM

LEAD SINGER!

NO PROBLEM!

100

NOD NOD

OH?

RIGHT. HI, KURAI-SAN.

YOU'RE THE VEHICLE, TOO?

WE'VE GOT SOME TIME SO LET'S PRACTICE.

TAP

THUMP THUMP THUMP THUMP

-SPORTS EST IS... ESOME. ♡

WOW, I'M HOLDING HANDS WITH AYANO-CHAN. ♡

WHOSE FAULT IS IT?

WHY THE SAD FACE? I'M COUNTING ON YOU AS MY VEHICLE.

WHAT'S UP, KAMIODA?

I MUST BE PUNCTUAL TO SUCCEED.

I'VE BEEN ASKED BY THE PRINCIPAL TO COORDINATE THE HALLOWEEN EVENT.

KAMIODA-KUN.

WE NEED TO TALK.

WAIT.

H-HEY!

APPLE

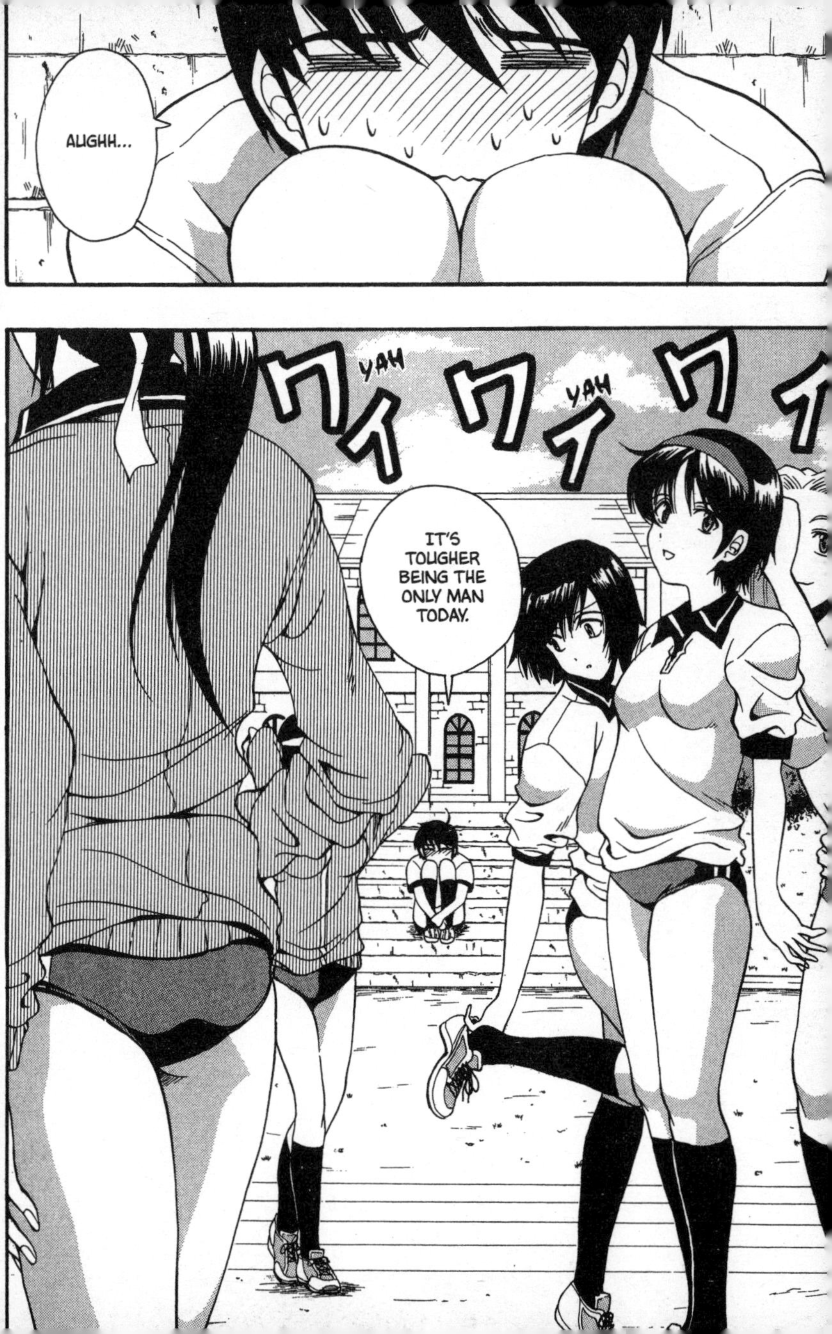
AUGHH...
ワイワイワイワイ
YAH
YAH
IT'S TOUGHER BEING THE ONLY MAN TODAY.

NO.

SHAKE

SHAKE

...

NOPE. ♪

It's a book....

HUH?

I'M GLAD THAT YOU'RE NOT AS TERRIFIED OF MEN NOW.

THANKS TO YOU.

THAT PARADE GAVE ME A PERFECT IDEA.

HEY, ORIMIYA-SAN!

A delayed reaction?

SWOO....

YOU DIDN'T KNOW? I WAS NEXT TO YOU WHEN YOU WERE REPAIRING THE WING.

OH NO.

OK, I GOT IT PERFECT NOW!

YOU'RE WELCOME.

THANKS, ORIMIYA-SAN!

FLINCH

You're saying that...

...even now?

UGH...

THEY CAME TO SEE THIS.

OH, I G IT NO

RIGHT, AND THAT'S WHAT I CAME FOR.

RIP

CRACK

EH?!

THAT'S IT!

THIS IS THE EVENT WE'RE AIMING FOR!

CLENCH

INVOLVING THE AUDIENCE AS WELL.

THE LIVING DEAD AND DEVILS DANCING FOR HALLOWEEN.

BUT WE CAN'T REALLY SEE FROM HERE!

OH, MY GOD! KAMIODA FELL TOWARD HER!

KAMIODA-KUN...

"MEN ARE ALL BEASTS."

"MEN ARE ALL..." BEASTS."

TREMBLE TREMBLE

I-I'M SORRY! ARE YOU ALL RIGHT?

THEY'RE ON THE FERRIS WHEEL.

WOW, IT'S MORE CRAMPED THAN I EXPECTED.

HEAVEN

RATTLE...

RATTLE...

UH, ARE YOU ALL RIGHT?

Y-YES.

I FEEL LIKE WE'RE DOING AN ENDURANCE TEST NOW.

THIS IS TURNING OUT STRANGE.

66

NOT ONLY THAT, THEY MAINTAIN A CONSISTENT DISTANCE BETWEEN THEM.

THEY HAVEN'T TRIED TO HOLD HANDS.

...BUT NOTHING LIKE THIS EVER HAPPENED.

YOU KNOW WE'VE WITNESSED MANY DATES...

YES, YES.

MUNCH MUNCH

CRUNCH CRUNCH

THIS IS JUST MY SPECU-LATION.

SHE IS SHARP!

SO SHE WENT ON A DATE WITH KAMIODA TO OVERCOME IT.

THAT'S ABOUT IT.

SHE MUST HAVE TROUBLE BEING AROUND GUYS.

Wonderland Coupon

Ferris Wheel

Valid only on date of issue

HMMM.

MUNCH MUNCH

CRUNCH CRUNCH CRUNCH!

Wonderland

IT'S FINE IF I CAN GIVE HER A HAND.

ALL I HAVE TO DO IS GET ON THE FREE RIDES AND HELP HER OVERCOME HER FEAR OF MEN.

I FEEL STRANGELY NERVOUS.

WE'RE ONLY WATCHING THE HALLOWEEN PARADE.

55

WHY ARE YOU TERRIFIED OF MEN?

I'VE BEEN WONDERING ABOUT THIS.

HMM? I WONDER WHERE MAMIYA-SAN WENT.

MY FATHER TAUGHT ME ABOUT MEN FROM A VERY YOUNG AGE.

OH...

HE TAUGHT YOU?

LIKE WHAT?

...

W-WELL...

HE SAID MEN ARE...

UMM...

53

SO I DON'T REALLY UNDERSTAND IT.

WELL, I JUST RANDOMLY PICKED THIS JOB,

HA HA HA.

LOOKS LIKE IT'S JUST THE TWO OF US NOW.

TAP TAP

ON TOP OF THAT, I'M INEXPERIENCED AT ORGANIZING PEOPLE.

I GUESS IT MEANS I SHOULDN'T ACCEPT SOMETHING I'M NOT FAMILIAR WITH.

TO THE ROOFTOP OF THE MAIN BUILDING.

HUH?

WANT TO GO TO THE ROOFTOP?

SCOOT

49

BAM

...

PANIC PANIC

AH!

42

HOW BORING.

AH, YES, IT'S PICASSO.

SO THERE'S NOTHING DIRTY ABOUT IT.

スリサリサリーリ

HSSSS

THANKS FOR YOUR HELP, MOCHIZUKI-SAN.

I WAS ABLE TO CREATE A GREAT PIECE OF ART.

KAMIODA-KUN?

DON'T WORRY ABOUT HALLOWEEN. ♡

AND THANKS TO YOU, KAMIODA-SAN. ♡

WOW!

WELL, YES...

THAT WAS FAST. DID YOU FIND SOMEONE?

UGH...

NO WAY! REALLY?

Y-YES.

YOU DID ALREADY?!

CHECK IT OUT. HE SAID HE FOUND SOMEBODY.

ANYWAY, I'LL HAVE TO EXPLAIN IT TO AYANO-CHAN PRIVATELY.

WELL, IT'S THAT GIRL IN THE ART CLUB.

SHE SEEMED TO HAVE CHANGED HER MIND.

AGH... WHAT SHOULD I DO ABOUT THE NUDE MODELING?

HMM.

AGAPE

AGAPE

I-IN THE NUDE?

WE WILL BE IN TOUCH.

I-I BETTER TELL THEM THE NEWS FIRST!

DASH DASH

DASH DASH

B-BUT SHE SAID THEY WILL HELP US!!

HOW CAN I EXPLAIN TO HER THE TERMS OF THIS AGREEMENT?

OH, YOU'RE BACK.

BUT THE PROBLEM IS...

BAM

28

I DON'T REALLY FEEL LIKE DOING THIS.

BUT I DON'T WANT ANYONE ELSE IN OUR CLUB.

...TERUMI SAIKO WILL ENDURE ANYTHING!

IF THIS WILL MAKE HER HAPPY...

IT'S ALL ABOUT REIKO ISSHIKI!

RAHH! THIS IS ALL FOR MISS REIKOOO!!

Secret Garden

Ooh, Miss Reiko! ♡

Thanks, Saiko-chan. Here is your reward. ♡

WE SHOULDN'T HAVE TURNED THEM AWAY BECAUSE WE ARE BUSY.

I'M SO SORRY, MISS REIKO! I WILL FREE OUR SCHEDULE FOR THEM!

THEY THOUGHT THEY COULD COUNT ON US.

OH, MY!

I HAVE UPSET MISS REIKO.

WHAT HAVE I DONE?

JEEZ, THEY INTERRUPTED MY PRECIOUS TIME WITH MISS REIKO.

Go away.

CAN'T WE POSSIBLY HELP THEM, SAIKO-SAN?

MISS REIKO, LET'S CONTINUE WHERE WE LEFT OFF. ♡

EH?

THEY CAME TO US BECAUSE THEY LIKED OUR WORK.

WELL, UM, WE'D LIKE TO ASK FOR YOUR ASSISTANCE.

ASSISTANCE?

HMM...

...WHICH IS THE EXACT TYPE OF DESIGN WE NEED.

WE SAW A FAIRYTALE-LIKE PAINTING AMONG THEM...

BAH

WE LOOKED AT YOUR DISPLAY IN THE HALLWAY

UH... YES.

SO YOU WANT US TO DO THE TOTAL DESIGN OF THE STAGE?

TWITCH

AH!

SHE
WOULD
PAINT
THEM.

SLOP

I WOULD
OFFER MY
ENTIRE BE-
ING TO HER
FOR THE
SAKE OF
ART.

DON'T
LOOK
AWAY.

JUST LOOK
AT MY BODY.

Look at me.

AS IF TO CARESS MY BODY, SHE WOULD TAKE HER BRUSH...

...AND CHOOSE THE SUITABLE COLORS...

...AND PAINT.

SLOP

EVERY HUMILIATING OR NEVER-SEEN-BEFORE PART OF ME.

...AND PAINT.

STARE

SHE WOULD TAKE THE BEST AND WORST PARTS OF MY BODY...

SPENDING AN AFTERNOON WITH MISS REIKO.

YES.

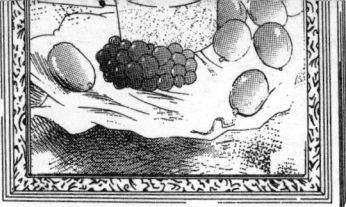

YES, I ASSUMED THEY ONLY DID STILL-LIFE, BUT I CAN TELL THEY'RE PUTTING EFFORT INTO OTHER STYLES, TOO.

AND THEY HAVE A KEEN SENSE OF COLOR.

THESE ARE GREAT PAINTINGS.

LET'S ASK THE CLUB!

I THINK THEY CAN HANDLE THE STAGE DESIGN FOR HALLOWEEN.

THEY HAVE A WIDE RANGE, FROM NATURALISM TO POP ART.

ART CLUB

#21 SECRET GARDEN

PURI PURI

contents

THIS IS A WORK OF FICTION.

MASATO KAMIODA

THE ONLY MALE STUDENT AT SAINT SOPHIA'S GIRLS' SCHOOL, HE WANTS TO BECOME A PRIEST. HE HAS FEELINGS FOR AYANO.

YOKO KURAI

MEMBER OF THE MONASTIC COUNCIL'S CHOIR CLUB. SHE PLAYS A BASS GUITAR.

MAI ORIMIYA

PRESIDENT OF THE MONASTIC COUNCIL'S SEWING CLUB AND A FIRST-YEAR STUDENT. SHE HAS A FEAR OF MEN.

SHE PLAYS DRUMS.

NONOKO AKARUI

PLOT SUMMARY

MASATO KAMIODA MAKES A CONCERTED EFFORT TO BECOME A PRIEST, TRAINING AT AN ALL-GIRLS DIVINITY SCHOOL. HE HAS COMPLETED MANY SUBJECTS IN THE PRIESTHOOD TRACK, BUT HE IS NOW DESIGNATED BY THE PRINCIPAL TO ACT AS THE COORDINATOR OF A HALLOWEEN FESTIVAL. HOWEVER, THE PRESIDENT OF THE CHOIR CLUB CHOOSES AN INAPPROPRIATE SONG TO PERFORM AND THE PRESIDENT OF THE SEWING CLUB IS TERRIFED OF MEN, MAKING PREPARATIONS DIFFICULT. WILL KAMIODA SUCCEED IN LAUNCHING THIS EVENT?!

AYANO MOCHIZUKI

KAMIODA-KUN'S CLASSMATE. SHE IS A COMPASSIONATE GIRL, LOOKING AFTER KAMIODA IN MANY WAYS. WHAT ARE HER INTENTIONS?

RIRISU MAMIYA

PRESIDENT OF THE MONASTIC COUNCIL'S CHOIR CLUB AND AN ENERGETIC GIRL DEVOTED TO ROCK MUSIC.

ERI GOTOKUJI

KAMIODA-KUN'S CLASSMATE. SHE THINKS HE IS A TOY.

CAPTAIN OF THE MONASTIC COUNCIL'S ORDER OF THE TEMPLAR AND AN EXCHANGE STUDENT. SHE IS GOOD WITH SWORDS BUT IS TERRIFIED OF GHOSTS.

SHERRICE D'ARC

RUMI ICHIJO

ERI'S BEST FRIEND AND CLASSMATE. SHE IS A PRANKSTER.

5

PURI PURI

Taro Chiaki

PURI PURI

Author Chiaki Taro
Translator Elina Ishikawa-Curran
Production Artist Taiwan production team
Production Manager Bryce Gunkel
English Adaptation Ailen Lujo
Editor Mike Stevens
Supervising Editor Gayle Tan
V.P. of Operations Yuki Chung
President Jennifer Chen

PURI PURI volume 5
© Chiaki Taro 2006

Originally published in Japan in 2006 by Akita Publishing Co., Ltd.
English translation rights arranged with Akita Publishing Co., Ltd. through
TOHAN CORPORATION, Tokyo.

PURI PURI volume 5
English translation © 2008 DrMaster Publications Inc.
All rights reserved.

DrMaster Publications Inc.
4044 Clipper Ct.
Fremont, CA 94538
www.DrMasterbooks.com

First Edition: April 2008

ISBN: 978-1-59796-105-9